work smarter
live better

Tina Konstant and Morris Taylor

Hodder Education
338 Euston Road, London NW1 3BH.

Hodder Education is an Hachette UK company

First published in UK 2011 by Hodder Education.

This edition published 2011.

Copyright © Tina Konstant and Morris Taylor

British Library Cataloguing in Publication Data: a catalogue record for this title
is available from the British Library.

10 9 8 7 6 5 4 3 2 1

The publisher has used its best endeavours to ensure that any website
addresses referred to in this book are correct and active at the time of going
to press. However, the publisher and the author have no responsibility for the
websites and can make no guarantee that a site will remain live or that the
content will remain relevant, decent or appropriate.

The publisher has made every effort to mark as such all words which it
believes to be trademarks. The publisher should also like to make it clear that
the presence of a word in the book, whether marked or unmarked, in no way
affects its legal status as a trademark.

Every reasonable effort has been made by the publisher to trace the copyright
holders of material in this book. Any errors or omissions should be notified in
writing to the publisher, who will endeavour to rectify the situation for any
reprints and future editions.

Hachette UK's policy is to use papers that are natural, renewable and
recyclable products and made from wood grown in sustainable forests.
The logging and manufacturing processes are expected to conform to the
environmental regulations of the country of origin.

www.hoddereducation.co.uk

Typeset by MPS Limited, a Macmillan Company.
Printed in Great Britain by CPI Cox & Wyman, Reading.

Contents

1   What is information overload and how do you
    know if you have it?   2

2   How do you cope with stress caused by information
    overload?   12

3   How do you avoid information overload at work?   24

4   How do you avoid information overload at home?   34

5   How do you manage written information?   42

6   How do you deal with verbal overload?   54

7   How to remember what you need to remember   66

8   How do you live life – not just survive day by day?   80

what is information overload and how do you know if you have it?

Information overload is an easy trap to fall into because on the surface, it seems like the problem comes from the world around you: people overload you; work overloads you; family overloads you; the media, the Internet and advertising overloads you. It's not your fault.

On closer inspection however, all the world is offering you is information and opportunity. What you choose to do with that information or that opportunity, or how well you tolerate the pressures associated with it, is what determines how overloaded you are.

The key word to remember as you go through this book is choice. As impossible as it sometimes seems, you always have a choice; stay or go, do something or do nothing. The degree to which you feel you cannot choose is the degree of overload you will experience. But what exactly is information overload and how do you know if you have it?

What is information overload?

Overload is a matter of perspective. The severity is determined by your perception of the consequences of not dealing with excess information. Some people deal with uncontrolled information (even if the consequences of ignoring it seem severe) because they have a higher panic threshold than others.

Information overload doesn't happen in isolation. If your life is in control then you will be able to manage vast amounts of new, unexpected, conflicting or challenging information. It will seem to you that your mind is open and able to cope with anything new – you are happy, calm and in control. If however, your life takes a turn and one area becomes uncontrolled – family, marriage, relationships, money – your ability to *cope* with new information will be suddenly and dramatically reduced.

In the Japanese martial art of aikido, you learn that when someone grabs you by the wrist that it is only that part of you that they control. You can still move the rest of your body. Treat information in the same way.

The small part of your life that seems out of control can momentarily blind you to the real scale of your problem. The trouble is, when you experience the emotional feelings that often go with overload, the pieces of information become attached to those feelings along with the potential of too many overbearing consequences. If you gain perspective over the problem and take control, your perception will change and so will your environment.

The purpose of information

How we perceive information and what we decide to do with it determines whether our lives are run by it or whether we are in control. Information can strengthen and secure our position at work. At home, information allows our family to control their lives. Information can also lead to independent wealth. We can have access to all the information the world has to offer, but if we don't use it appropriately, it becomes overload.

The symptoms of information overload

Apparent memory difficulties: Small things slip your mind. You get through the day but can't remember, at the end of the day, what you did at the beginning of it. You can't remember the names of people you have just met. You have difficulty recalling details, facts and figures. You have conversations during which you tend to 'zone out' and you find yourself unable to contribute because you literally didn't hear or take in what anyone was saying.

Easily distracted: You find yourself daydreaming or going blank for periods of time. Your mind leaps from one subject to another with no apparent connection between the subjects. You start sentences and conversations but don't finish them. You start projects and tasks but don't finish them. Everything gets your attention and you find it difficult to concentrate for long periods of time.

Worry: Your time may be taken up with concerns and fears about what you might be missing or what you should be doing. You worry about what other people are doing and about how what you're not doing will affect them. You might also worry about what people think of your competence or your ability to do your job. You might become uncomfortable during meetings because you feel you're behind everyone else and are paranoid that everyone knows.

Over-compensation: Even though you know you can't keep up you might take on even more in the belief you will give the illusion of being in control. Trouble is, if you're not in control, the more you take on, the less you can do. To hide that you're in trouble you might talk a lot but deliver little, especially if the tasks are either difficult or outside your skill range. Instead of halting the situation and allowing a re-evaluation, you might start a series of conversations intended to delay delivery. This shares the load by passing information (or non-information) to others so that it becomes impossible for you to complete the task because 'you're waiting for Joe Doe to get back to you'. You've created gateways so that others have to do non-work before you can do the real work. This widely used tactic shifts blame on to all the other people you pulled into those conversations. Effectively, what you say is: 'I couldn't do this task because Joe Doe didn't get back to me with this particular infinitesimal piece of useless information.' By then those around you are so confused that they've forgotten the original scope of the job, it goes beyond what they feel they should be doing or gets handed off to someone else.

Stress: This leads to over-eating, under-eating, too much sleep, too little sleep, extremes of everything and is one of the key indicators of overload. This is covered in more detail in Chapter 2.

Procrastination: When you have so much to do that you can't decide what to do, you will do nothing. Many people wait until a situation becomes critical. They deal with what is urgent, when it's urgent, and only because it's urgent. As well as adding to stress, procrastination can lead to the overwhelming feeling of being out of control. Procrastinators forget that they're in a perpetual state of emergency because they've sat for days or weeks in a state of worry and fear. If they had taken action sooner, they would not have to deal with any emergency and they probably wouldn't be overloaded. Procrastination is not only a symptom of overload, it is one of the direct causes. However, not all procrastination is bad. Sometimes it's a signal from your brain that you've missed something important and you shouldn't take another step until you've identified it and dealt with it.

Frozen: This happens when you are feeling so overloaded you can't cope. When you reach this stage you become incapable of doing anything. You don't think, you don't act, you don't respond to what's going on around you. You feel numb and apparently oblivious to the consequences of your inaction. Despite the urgency you not only do nothing but you feel nothing. You pass the load to someone else who may have noticed that you're overloaded. If no one has noticed, they soon will when a deadline is missed. Regardless of the consequences, you will still have done nothing.

Anatomy of information overload

The chain of warning signs looks like this:

1 **Life is good.** You're generous with your time and frequently say things like 'sure, I can do that' to any request. You're feeling good. The world is in order.

2 **Requests increase because you're a 'can-do' individual.** Information flows your way and you begin to notice a slight sense of unease. You ignore it but start avoiding certain people or certain topics of conversation.

3 **Work stacks up.** You notice that you don't open all your mail every day. Emails stack up. Your mental attitude is still good: 'I'll catch up on Saturday. Kids can look after themselves. It'll only take an hour or so.'

4 Gradually, **weekends, evenings and holidays turn in to catch-up times.**

5 **A rift forms between professional and personal life.** You don't want your family and friends to suffer because you have a 'bit too much on your plate', so instead of spending a couple of hours catching up, you sneak time here and there to do what you have to do. You feel bad because you're not being totally honest with your family or with yourself. But you do what you have to do.

6 Instead of sneaking time at home, you decide you'd get a lot more done, a lot quicker, if you stayed at work a little longer. So you do. **Your hours extend.** First evenings, then Saturday morning, then all day Saturday.

7 **People around you are annoyed because 'you're always at work'.** You get annoyed because they're annoyed: 'I have to. I have no choice. It's my job.'

8 **Tension builds at home and in your social life.** You start to go to work to get away from it all. But you're tired and frustrated. Overload increases. Cracks show. Your behaviour changes. People at work notice that you're snappy, disorganized, late for meetings. Trouble is, you've said yes to so many people and projects that your commitments prevent you from backing

out. You're in a moral catch-22: you said yes to be helpful and professional but your desire to continue to be helpful and professional is preventing you from regaining control over your environment.

9 **Your mind crosses a line and you shut down.** You step into your office after working all weekend and having had a fight at home. You open emails. Glance down at the stacked in-tray. There's another request from someone. It's not a big request. The deadline isn't that urgent. They probably wouldn't mind if you said 'no' (although they would be surprised because you've said 'yes' to everyone else).

10 **Information overload hits you square in the face.** You can't see wood for trees and you have bark embedded in your forehead to prove it. Suddenly, you're out of control and don't know what to do next.

What to do next

If you feel that your mind is about to collapse under the strain, step out of the 'overload' environment – home or office. This includes temporarily distancing yourself from anyone you think may be contributing to your feelings of overload – friends, family, colleagues.

Your initial reaction to this may be: 'I can't!! I have too much to do!! My family/colleagues need me!! I'm a mum/dad with responsibilities!! I can't just take time out!!' The alternative is to carry on you are.

Your don't have to take a week out of your life; just a few hours – maybe a day at most.

Take a clean, new notepad and a pen. Leave everything else behind: briefcase, bag and all the clutter you carry with you. Find a place where you can sit and think – teashop, park, anywhere. Take a little time to put what's going on around you in perspective by answering the following questions:

1 What part of your life is currently not working – work, money or family? Remember, we're dealing with information overload and not general life fixing. Focus only on work, family or money – three areas where overload tends to congregate.

2 Which part of your environment is the most cluttered – home, work or both?

3 Of the areas you've identified, which do you feel most emotional about? Where do you feel most angry, frustrated or sad? Many other factors can contribute to feelings of anger, frustration or sadness, so think only in terms of information overload. After you have information in control, and reduced the emotional effects of overload, other things may change too.

4 Once you've identified what overloads you, list all the people in that environment who contribute to that overload – friends, family, colleagues, bosses.

5 Next to each person's name, write down what you think their expectations of you are. What do your children expect? What does your boss expect? Your creditors? Your bank manager? Your colleagues? Don't take the easy way out and just say 'everything'. Break it down. Ask yourself what each person in your life *specifically* expects of you.

6 When you have that list for each person in your life, take the time to be honest and reasonable with yourself. Ask yourself what is genuine and what is self-inflicted. Are you the mental and physical store house for everyone's schedules? Does that work for you? Is it causing you to burn out? Is it possible for each person to be responsible for their own schedule? What would happen if they were? What if you weren't responsible for other people's lives? What if they took responsibility?

7 When you have your list of true and reasonable expectations (personal and professional), list all the information you're currently dealing with to satisfy each of those expectations: schedules, bills, banking, tasks, projects, deadlines.

You should now have a list of all the main people in your life. Those who, as well as contributing to your sense of wellbeing, may overload you, perhaps without intending to. Each person's expectations will be divided between what is real and what is self-inflicted. All your current tasks, deadlines and activities associated with each of those expectations should also be listed.

It's important that you're honest with and about yourself. Not being honest will mean that as you begin to untangle the overload, you'll be focusing on the wrong information. You might focus on your job where in fact, it's not that. It may be that monthly bills are actually causing the overload. If you focus only on your job, you'll feel pressure and just work harder (but not necessarily smarter) and not focus on the fact that your finances are in disarray – 'I'm working as hard as I can! What more can I do?' doesn't fly with credit cards and bank managers. Your greatest enemy is denial.

Now comes either the really easy part, or the truly difficult part – it all depends on what's on your list.

8 If you experience overload at work, at home and in your finances, prioritize them by determining which has the greatest consequence if ignored. Deal with that first. You won't be ignoring the other areas of your life. You'll just be dealing with the tough one first.

Working on trivia is okay if you are the only person affected by your overload. It makes you feel busy and, for a while, there are no great consequences. The real issues start when your overload affects the outside world – especially the world of finance, government, business colleagues, friends and family. When your overload makes those people unhappy, you will have a problem you can't ignore.

If your finances are in disarray, every envelope will fill you with dread. Your behaviour towards simple daily tasks will change. You won't answer phone calls. Won't open the mail. You refuse to acknowledge the problem. This is simple denial. But just because you're ignoring the situation, it doesn't mean anyone else is.

When information overload is a good excuse

Do you like to feel overloaded? Does it make you feel important? Do you secretly enjoy being the person in the office with so much to do that you have to come into the office at 6 a.m.

and can only leave at 8 p.m? Does it make you feel indispensable? Do you care that people notice that you come in early and go home late? You are unlikely to admit this to anyone except yourself (and even that might not be possible) but do you find relief in being able to tell your family that you can't do certain things with them because you're too overloaded at work and you need to work late or work over the weekend in order to catch up? Do you use the 'too much to do' excuse to avoid things you don't want to do?

If so, you're doing one of two things:

* You're **consciously** making up overload so you can use it as an excuse to get out of doing what you don't want to do or being where you don't want to be.
* You're **unconsciously** making up overload so you can use it as an excuse to get out of doing what you don't want to do or being where you don't want to be.

Either way, you need to take the time to understand what you are trying to avoid and what damage you are doing to yourself, your family, your social life and your job by making yourself appear too busy to deal with the important stuff in your life.

If you don't, people will eventually stop asking you to join in. They will assume you are too busy and when you decide you need to rejoin the world, it might not be so easy.

How to deal with overload when it's not 'just in your head'

Sometimes overload is not just in your head. Sometimes it is very real and takes the form of paper, emails, books, deadlines, visual and auditory noise.

It is vital to keep a clear head and maintain perspective no matter how much apparent overload you're collapsing under. I say apparent, because you are the one who has decided you're overloaded. Other people may load you up with work and information, but you have flipped the mental switch from control to chaos.

2

how do you cope with stress caused by information overload?

All stress, if you think about it, is related in some way to information overload; everything from feeling overwhelmed by financial responsibility to being the first on the scene of an accident. As hard as it might be to accept however, regardless of the situation, stress is self-inflicted and based entirely on your perception of the events going on around you. As a result, the best way to manage it is to learn to trust your intuition when making decisions and respond calmly and logically to your environment.

Easier said than done? The techniques in this chapter take only a moment to do. The more you practise them, the more benefit you will feel. Use them on a regular basis because whether or not the overload is genuine, the stress symptoms you experience are real and if left unaddressed will cause serious damage in the long term.

Clear your head when pressure is at its peak

There are thinking cells in your kidneys, liver, heart and gut that are identical to the cells that make up your brain. Your body is populated with thinking cells. As a result, gut feelings, butterflies in your stomach, prickles in your neck and heartfelt feelings are more than mere sensations. Your body is like a radar system, constantly picking up information from your environment. It's never overloaded. It delegates. It notices what's important and ignores the rest. When something requires your attention (impending danger for instance) your body gives you a combination of physical and emotional messages. These messages are sometimes in the form of a feeling or 'little voices' and are often ignored. Yet, as well as help you make the right decision, they can save your life.

The more you understand and trust your instincts (as opposed to reacting instinctively), the easier it will be to make clear and accurate decisions in difficult situations. The more in touch you are with your body, the easier it will be to understand the information it gives you.

Listen to your heart

Any time you feel stressed, overloaded or are faced with a difficult situation or decision:

1 Think about the decision or event or situation you want to handle.
2 Breathe and focus your attention on your feet, then your knees, then your hands. Notice any sensations in those areas.
3 Focus your attention on the area of your chest surrounding your heart.
4 Imagine what it would be like if you were able to breathe through your heart. We know you can't, so just *pretend*. Imagine if air did not pass through your mouth, nose and lungs, if that whole area was silent and instead, you could breathe, clearly and fully, directly with your heart.
5 After a while, recall a time you experienced true appreciation. Recall who was there, and what it felt like.

6 Recall that feeling and, when you have it back, go back to your heart.

7 Ask your heart how it would handle the situation or decision you are finding difficult.

8 Pay attention to the answer and notice any sensations, emotions or feelings.

9 Make a decision on what you are going to do next.

The above may take a few minutes the first time you try it. After you have done it a few times you can *begin* by breathing with your heart. It is one of the quickest ways of reducing stress in any situation.

Use your senses

This needs two people. It is wonderful to do with children. Use a blindfold to inhibit vision. The blindfolded person will be presented with a variety of stimuli – touch, sound, taste or smell. The purpose is to encourage the blindfolded person to describe what they hear, smell, taste or feel by describing the *pictures* they see in their heads when they are presented with the stimulus. If you put their hand on a warm radiator for instance, they cannot simply say, 'it's warm'. Encourage them to describe what 'warm' might look like if they turned it into a picture. If they cannot find a picture immediately, start at the edge, asking them to describe what colour it might be, then what shape, then any movement and gradually, from the images, a picture of the feeling will emerge. The key here is *safety* and *permission*. As soon as someone puts a blindfold on they trust you. Don't present them with anything alive (even if it's a family pet) or anything that might harm or startle them (for example, anything too hot or too cold). The more relaxed the blindfolded person is, the easier it will be to generate visual images. And remember, it'll be your turn next!

Regain your perspective

Once you have managed your stress, maintain your wellbeing by regaining your perspective. The world is what it is: madness, aggression, peace, harmony, contradictions, differences and overload. It is your *perception* that determines whether it is chaos and disorder or sense and order. Think of a busy airport, people rushing everywhere, bumping and complaining, looking lost and bewildered. It's hot, your bags are heavy, everything is in chaos. You become tense and before you know it, you would rather you weren't taking any trip to any exotic island. Step back for a second. Take a look at the scene. Don't try to push and shove your way through people. Take your time, breathe and relax. Take the events for what they are. Just a busy airport. Your mood begins to change, people seem to smile more. Anticipation replaces frustration. In a moment, the chaos becomes excitement and fun. Airports are start points of adventure. For the most part, they are exciting places. A change in perspective allows you to experience a different world, one free from anger, frustration, fear and debilitating tension.

Consider another example. Wars are fought because two sides have different views of who is right and who is wrong. People inflict the most horrific acts on each other believing they are perfectly justified and right in doing so. What is terrorism to one cultural viewpoint is the justified action of a 'freedom fighter' to another. How do you persuade one side to acknowledge and appreciate the sentiments of the other? Our perceptions are not only ingrained in our conscious thoughts but they are in our unconscious behaviours that come from generations of behaviour and belief.

Dealing with information in a calm, balanced state allows you to change some of your ingrained thinking. You have the opportunity to consider someone else's perspective before making a judgement. It also means that when stress and negative responses to a situation are simply making matters worse you have the skills required to stop, slow down, change your perspective and see things in a more constructive light.

Practise perspective

This exercise can be done wherever you have some time to play – sitting at a bus stop, having a cup of tea somewhere or attending a meeting that is proving to be uninteresting!

Notice an event or activity going on around you at the time. An event containing some tension works best: an argument between two people; a parent struggling with a moody child; a waiter managing a tricky customer – anything that has the potential for a less than positive ending. Imagine you were *part* of the event. How would you manage it? Next, imagine you were one of the people involved in the event, or a world leader or someone else entirely. How would you manage that event if you were someone else? Step into their shoes, think of what these different people would have to consider in responding to the event. What would you bring to the event that they could not?

Look for reasons why the event should or should not be taking place. Look for reasons why each person might be right or wrong. Look for justification for each person's actions. Look at the event from every perspective possible. Practise this often, play with it and then take it seriously when you are in a position of conflict.

Two important notes to remember:
* Although you might be able to appreciate another person's perspective, you don't have to agree.
* A person's actions *always, always, always* make perfect sense to them.

Respond to stress and change perspective on overload

Stress happens either when your situation outweighs your perceived ability to deal with it, or worse still, when you are overloaded without realizing it. This perception will vary day to day, moment to moment. 'Perception' is the operative word. You might have no more to do on Tuesday than you had on Monday, but because your mood or environment is different, what you have to do might seem more than it really is, and the perception that you cannot cope will increase regardless of the reality of your current surroundings.

A number of stressors can affect your ability to perceive the world in a calm, balanced way:

* **Environment** – noise, chaos and pollution
* **Social** – people, deadlines, financial problems
* **Physiological** – aches, pains, poor nutrition, lack of exercise

By far the most dominant and potentially damaging are:

* **Your own thoughts** – it is the *interpretations* that we place on a situation that generate stress. As Shakespeare says, 'There is nothing either good or bad, but thinking makes it so' (Hamlet).

Re-interpret stress

Break the routine

It is important you pay attention to the messages your body brings to your conscious awareness and that you act on that information. Your body is hormone driven and works on a cycle throughout the day. When you feel like you need a cup of tea or coffee, or you start yawning or making mistakes, your body is telling you it is time to stop and rest (see Ernest Rossi's book *The 20 Minute Break*). The longer you put off having a break, the more difficult it will be to get back to work after you finally decide to take one. If you have a lot to do, it is better to take plenty of little breaks and small snacks during the day rather than work through the whole morning, stop for a full lunch and then suffer in the afternoon.

Carrot or stick

One way to encourage yourself to keep your mind open and your perspectives clear is to reward yourself. If you work in a conventional environment you may not feel that you are fully recognized or rewarded for your efforts. Instead of waiting for a reward for your work to come from somewhere else, take responsibility for giving yourself a reward. At the beginning of the day determine the things you are going to accomplish and what your rewards will be (*not* sweets and sugars – this only rewards the taste buds!). Vary your rewards. Choose things that are good for you, things you really want: anything ranging from an evening in a steam room to a proper holiday for finishing a big project on time. Have plenty of reasons to treat yourself. You will feel happier, your motivation will increase and your stress levels will reduce.

Anti-ostrich policy

Maintain an anti-ostrich policy. Being open-minded and receptive to new ideas will make your day more creative and problem free. If you avoid sticking your head in the sand you will be aware of what is going on around you and on the look out for potential problems and their solutions. Potential problems only *become* real and unmanageable when they are ignored. Keep your head out of the sand and your mind open. When you no longer fear managing difficult issues, they won't seem so big. Fear of problems makes them worse. Treat problems for what they are – a series of events that you have to disentangle. Remember, however, the other extreme: 'hyper vigilance'. That can be just as damaging albeit in a different way.

Rid yourself of clutter and confusion

An environment you can and must control is your workspace. Every piece of paper on your desk will attract your attention several times a day. If each piece of paper had a deadline attached to it, you would have a desk full of alarm clocks sounding off every five minutes alerting you to the pressure you are under, interrupting your concentration, inducing chronic stress and causing long-term damage to your *capacity* to concentrate.

If you have a clear desk, your environment will look and feel in control. You may have a great deal to do but you will be able to tackle each task one at a time with a clear mind. The perception that your environment is out of control will diminish if it looks organized.

Your living space

This is not an exercise in Feng Shui, although Feng Shui is worth a look. Your living space is a reflection of your mind and thinking processes. Look at your home. Compare the state of your home and the state of your mind.

If you are happy with your living space, if you love going home, if you feel calm and peaceful, creative and relaxed in your living space, then your living space is right for you. If, on the other hand, you spend most of your time out because every time you go home you are reminded of chores you don't want to do then it may be worth taking some time to organize and clear your space so that you can live in it, rather than use your creative ability to generate excuses on how to avoid it.

The space you live in should be the one place in the world where you can just 'be'. If you have a big, chaotic family make sure you have at least *one* space and one time that is yours.

Exercises to reduce stress and maintain perspective

Breathing

Although most of your brain cells would die without oxygen within three to five minutes, you can live a whole lifetime without breathing *properly* and not be aware of it. Your body uses your breathing as a signal to tell you when something is wrong; when you are feeling stressed or threatened you feel it in your breathing. When you are tired, you yawn to take in more air. When you are in a room with poor ventilation it doesn't take long before you feel uneasy, get a headache or feel tired. These signals should not be ignored.

Correct breathing relieves a number of symptoms including stiffness, tension, irritability, headaches, fatigue and depression. Poor breathing habits considerably impact your ability to monitor stress and respond positively to events around you.

Several breathing exercises that don't take long to do and that you can do in any environment will help reduce stress. These exercises are easy to learn. Practise a breathing exercise several times every day at the same time or in response to a regular occurrence.

This will gradually become a routine and will help remind you that you have a choice when a situation gets out of hand.

Your body will soon learn to relax naturally, in a very few moments, when you are faced with a challenging situation that requires thought, an open mind and a shift in perspective.

This is a good breathing exercise if you don't want others around you to know you are doing it. At each in-breath make sure you are breathing into your abdomen rather than your chest. To check this (assuming you can't place your hands on your abdomen area to check whether it is moving or not), place your awareness around your waist and, as you breathe, you should feel a tightening around your clothing.

1 Exhale comfortably and take in a slow, deep breath and hold for the count of eight.
2 Slowly exhale.
3 Take three or four breaths like this and relax.
4 Accompany the breathing with a good stretch if you can.

If you have only a few minutes, this yoga breathing exercise is wonderful for relaxing and focusing.

1 Close your eyes for a few moments.
2 Place your right thumb on your right nostril and block it.
3 Breathe in deeply and slowly through your left nostril for six seconds.
4 Block both nostrils using your thumb and your middle finger and hold for six seconds.
5 Remove your thumb from your left nostril only and slowly exhale.
6 Pause for six seconds.
7 Then continue by breathing in through your left nostril, closing both, and exhaling through your right.
8 Continue to do this for as long as you feel comfortable.

If you are tired and you have much to do, this will help wake you up and increase alertness.

1 Stand or sit up straight.
2 Breathe abdominally.
3 Hold your breath for a count of six.

4 Purse your lips and blow out short bursts of air fairly forcefully until you have totally exhaled.

5 Breathe in deeply again and repeat the exercise several times.

Being present and in perspective

It is impossible (and undesirable) to be totally present and focused all the time. Imagination and creativity happens when your mind wanders beyond your present space and time. Sometimes, however, you need to be fully present and aware. This exercise will help you develop the necessary state of mind.

1 Sit or stand still for a moment.

2 First, close your eyes if you can and notice what you can hear. How many conversations can you make out? What are people saying? Can you hear any traffic? What is the furthest sound you can hear? What is the closest sound you can hear? What is the most familiar or the most foreign or unusual sound? What is the most or least pleasant sound? Describe every sound you can hear.

3 Next, notice what you can feel. How close are people to you? What does the floor feel like beneath your feet? What do your clothes feel like on you? Is there a breeze, if so, what direction is it coming from?

4 With your eyes open, notice the colours. How many different shades of red or blue or orange can you see? What is the most common colour in your view? What is the least common colour in your view? Now notice the shapes. If you observed your surroundings and had to describe them in terms of shapes only, and not what the objects really are how would you describe them?

5 Finally, appreciate your surroundings.

No matter how noisy or chaotic your present surroundings, when you *really* pay attention and be present you will be surprised at the level of comfort and relaxation you experience. This may simply be the result of knowing your surroundings for what they are instead of making interpretations.

Do this as often as you have time. Especially when you are feeling that your environment might be getting out of control.

Perspective experiment

Try this thought experiment or, provided you take sensible precautions, do it for real. You will need a group of people, a thermometer, and three pails of water: one pail very cold (almost freezing), another at room temperature (around 20°C), a third at about the temperature of the hottest bath you can safely tolerate. Each of you take turns: sit for a *short* time with your left hand in the cold water, at the same time as your right hand is in the 'hot' water, then put both hands into the room temperature water. You will notice that, although both hands are now immersed at the same temperature, the left hand feels that it is in hot water, while the right feels that it is in cold water. Different people will interpret a situation in entirely different ways based on their previous experience.

Your memories, experiences and attitudes build a mental model of the world that act as a filter on incoming information. Your senses – sight, hearing, touch – absorb *everything*. As new information passes through your senses into your brain, you make sense of it by fitting the information into your mental model. This filtering process means that you do not see the *real* world, rather, your interpretation of it.

3

how do you avoid information overload at work?

Most people say that the primary source of information overload is the office or wherever 'work' happens. This might or might not be true. What is true is that not all overload experienced in this environment is someone else's fault because the roots of overload at work are two habits that you have absolute control over: perfection and procrastination.

We all have an idea of what perfect is. Trouble is, your 'perfect' might be someone else's first draft. Perfection is a myth so get over it and move on. The other half to this pair is procrastination: 'I can't get it right; I don't know what to do, so I won't do anything at all.'

Perfection and procrastination march hand in hand through your day, each becoming an excuse for the other. In the mean time the world keeps moving; backing up deadlines, increasing overload and building stress.

Deal with self-inflicted information overload

Aiming for perfection only makes sense if, and only if, no one else will have an interest in the outcome. If others are going to have input, then a *compromise* is as good as you will get. For perfectionists, this may be difficult. But if a compromise is not made, the perfectionist will remain overloaded and continue to overload others with trivia.

The two main categories of perfectionist

1. Time perfectionists

People who will do *whatever* it takes to meet a deadline. Quality be damned, meet the deadline. This type of perfectionist will find shortcuts to ensure they meet deadlines, often with time to spare. They are so focused on completion that they miss opportunities and different alternatives. They don't take the time to explore options. Working with time-perfect people is also difficult because they are always rushing and creating mini deadlines throughout the project, instead of just letting the project flow. The overload this creates can be catastrophic to a project because the rest of the team won't know what is genuinely urgent and what is urgent only to the time perfectionist.

2. Quality perfectionists

People who will sacrifice time for quality. Their motto is, 'if you want it right, you'll have to wait'. The job is not complete until every aspect is checked, double checked and confirmed. The finished product might be perfect, however, as far as others are concerned, packed with flaws (especially if 'being on time' was one of the pre-conditions). This type of perfectionism can be a screen for lack of confidence. If you can't submit work because it's 'not finished/perfect', is it a lack of confidence, fear of disapproval, fear of failure or fear of success that stops you? Those who suffer from quality perfectionism don't believe that anyone can do the job as well as they can, and as a result do more work than would otherwise be necessary.

One of the greatest flaws of a perfectionist is that they don't believe that there is anything wrong with the way they work because they are … perfect. So, if you recognize yourself in one of these categories, and admit that perhaps the way you work is not 'perfect', then all is not lost.

Solutions

If you are time perfect

The balance that a time-perfect person needs to achieve is the one between quality and time. A time-perfect person needs to develop a sense of realism. They tend to give themselves heroic deadlines, without thinking about what actually has to be achieved. They then get fixated on the time instead of the outcome of the product and they overload themselves from the outset.

The following are some ideas on how you begin to achieve the balance between time and quality.

* When someone asks you how long it will take, pause, take a deep breath, think about what you would normally say, and then double or treble it. If you finish early, then great, but *be realistic*. Give yourself the time to think about quality as well.

* Learn to feel comfortable about extended deadlines. Some deadlines are flexible. There may be time to play with. Do this only once. If you do it too often you may lose credibility. Before you extend a deadline consider what happens to your work when you pass it on. If you extend the delivery date very far beyond the agreed date, it might cause difficulty and inconvenience for those who have to have input to your output.

* If you work in a team on a project and time is a critical factor, it is important to be very clear and honest with them about the deadlines and what needs to be achieved. Non-time-perfect people will be frustrated if they are given untrue deadlines. If there are ten weeks to complete a project and the time-perfect team leader tells the team

that there are in fact only eight weeks, the leader is putting the team in a position of completing what would normally take ten weeks in less than eight. This will undoubtedly have an impact on team performance, stress levels and quality of work. Also, if the team discover that they did in fact have ten weeks, they will lose faith in the leader who will find it very difficult to be taken seriously at a later date. Be honest and be realistic. People are quite capable of managing their own time; you don't have to do it for them.

* At the start of the project be honest with the team. Tell them exactly how much time they have to complete the project, create a plan highlighting key dates when parts of the project have to be completed. Make sure everyone has input into the plan and is aware of it.

If you are quality perfect

If you know a quality perfectionist, help them to widen their view of the world. It is important that they consider more than their own idea of a project outcome: perfect for one person does not mean perfect for another. Whether performance, writing, product design or construction, *always* have the audience in mind. Whose opinion really counts? Thousands of small, medium and large businesses fail every year because at some time they build their business around what *they* think is right rather than what the customer wants. Think of the end user. Think of the audience.

When balancing the possible and the perfect, it is important to have a good sense of when good is good enough. Things can always be better but improvement can only happen if there is something to improve on. If you don't close a project and put it into the world, you will never find out what your market would like to improve in it. Needs change and what was once 'perfect' becomes either inadequate or unwanted. What would have happened if Alexander Graham Bell had decided not to make the telephone public because it wasn't perfect, or Edison had kept the light bulb a secret because it wasn't quite bright enough? Perfection is a process. You rarely get there in a single step.

Achieving balance

'Fit for purpose' should be the new motto of recovering perfectionists. Make it perfect to the degree of 'fit for purpose'. This means that your work should:

* perform the job required
* suit the needs of end users and audiences
* be within time, budget and to specification
* be completed with minimum stress and frustration
* be open to continuous improvement: perfectionists are not keen to allow others to suggest improvements – if it's perfect there is no need for improvement, right?

There are times when perfection is not just necessary, it is a top priority, for example getting the maths perfect for a moon landing or the process exactly right in surgery. In most other cases perfectionism can be a hindrance. Striving for perfection first time round prevents you from trying alternative options, or experimenting.

To avoid overloading yourself and others, have the wisdom to decide when to be perfect, good, excellent, or not to care at all! The skill lies in knowing when perfection is the enemy of excellence.

Finish-lines – better than 'deadlines'

'Deadline' is a loaded word. It implies disaster if it isn't met, a bit like a 'Drop Dead Date'. The interesting thing about 'deadlines' is that often there are several attached to most large projects: the one stated at the start of the project, the one you impose on yourself, the one others impose on you, the real one and the delayed one. Be flexible and realistic, and if more time becomes available to complete a project, use it.

Time and pressure

Learn to love it. Controlled stress is healthy. Trouble arises when you have too much to do and you are not in control of it. The more you plan, the more control you will have over events, and the less negative stress you are likely to experience. Balance out stress with recovery time. Take a break, finish work on time, and don't let activity obstruct your sleep. If you are tired, even the most simple events can become disasters.

Thinking time and purpose

You can spend days and days 'doing'. But if you look closely at what you are doing, you might be surprised at how trivial most of it is. If you take time to think about what you want to do and how you want to do it, your time will have much more purpose and the events in your life will have much more meaning. Some of the most important and valuable time is the time you take to think and reflect.

What's the big deal about being late?

If you are late you are wasting someone else's time: that is disrespectful. Sometimes, it can't be helped, but let people know! Henry Ford said 'never complain, never explain'. If you are late, the person you are keeping waiting doesn't need to know all the intimate details of why you are late (unless it relates to them) and they most certainly don't need a made-up excuse. Keep it simple, keep it honest and don't make a habit of it. Being late all the time will only help you to develop a reputation for unreliability. Lateness increases stress for all involved. If you cancel all your other New Year resolutions, try to make this one stick: be on time.

Sometimes the best way to ensure an event fits into the time available is to take a break. Speed and action aren't always appropriate: stop and think.

Procrastination is another reason excess reading material accumulates. Two causes of procrastination are fear or lack of interest. If a task seems challenging you might do other seemingly important things instead of dealing with reality.

The cure is straightforward. Instead of imagining how bad a task might be, determine precisely what it entails. Get the facts. Then chunk the work into do-able pieces. Then do one piece at a time.

If the cause is lack of interest, find something about it that motivates you. If you find nothing and your desk is always full of paperwork but you just can't be bothered, consider negotiating your job description. Or find a different job!

Being a bottleneck achieves little. Information must flow freely in an organization. You will be surprised how much you can achieve when you enlist the help of others and share information.

Meetings and your time

Meetings can be one of the biggest time-wasters and anyone attending one can almost guarantee they will leave with more work than they went in with.

Saving time at meetings

* Have a clear agenda agreed by all parties up front.
* When writing the agenda, have three categories of topics:
  1 Topics that *have* to be discussed (vital and crucial).
  2 Topics that *should* be discussed (important but not vital).
  3 Any other business. Don't leave A.O.B. to the end of the meeting. It is the end of the day, people may be tired and (should be) wanting to get back to work. If there is too much A.O.B. the quality of discussion is not good. You will physically or mentally lose many of the attendees and there will be no definite time limit because the A.O.B. time is undefined. So, write the agenda, send it around and tell people to add any other business they want to include, then predetermine the time you will allow for A.O.B. If it is not included before the meeting, it doesn't get discussed.
* Start exactly on time. Don't recap for late comers.
* When you are chairing or facilitating a meeting the most important thing to do is to prevent time-wasters from taking over the agenda and waffling.
* Have someone take very clear and full notes. The person who takes the minutes should have some knowledge of the subject but should not be biased. The person who takes the notes should *not* be expected to contribute to the meeting.

* Set and adhere to times for oxygen breaks.
* Take a break at least every 90 minutes.
* At the start of the meeting, write up the exact agenda and the timing, i.e. points 1–4 before the first break, points 5–7 before the second break etc.
* As the meeting progresses, cross off the subjects covered. Don't retrace your steps.
* Always have a facilitator; it is their job to keep the meeting moving. If the meeting is large and long, get someone from outside the company. The facilitator, like the minute-taker, cannot take part in the discussion. The facilitator must be assertive, firm and respected by those attending. Timing is the facilitator's number one responsibility. If the meeting moves in such a way that it becomes clear that more discussion is needed, then it is the facilitator's responsibility to make any changes to the agenda to make sure the timing still works. The facilitator cannot be shy or shrinking. He or she must take control of the meeting from the very start.
* The chair is responsible for content, although the facilitator can help with this. As soon as delegates begin to waffle or go off subject, the chairperson (with the assistance of the facilitator) must get them back on subject. Waffling is one of the greatest of all time-wasters at meetings. Some people seem to make it their aim to speak rubbish at meetings. Make it clear, with a smile, at the beginning of the meeting that this will not be tolerated.
* Don't try to fit too much into any meeting.
* Don't run meetings for the sake of it. If you have a scheduled meeting every morning or every Friday, make sure there is a clearly understood, specific reason for it. Don't make meetings a habit.
* Full-day meetings are *never* as effective as those that last only a few hours. Keep them short and to the point.
* Don't invite known time-wasters to meetings unless you can contain them or use their talents.

* Don't make meetings open to anyone who wants to come unless necessary.
* Stop at the end of the meeting. The temptation is to carry it on in the halls outside the meeting. Once it's done, it's done.
* Make action come out of your meetings. Everyone must be clear about *what* exactly is to be done, *who* is to do it, *who* will follow up and *when* the follow-up will happen. People can be quick to agree to do something because it makes them look good; carrying it through is a different matter. The time that will be spent carrying out the actions arising from a meeting is more valuable than the time spent at the meeting.
* Don't waste anyone's time by creating senseless, unlimited or unallocated actions out of meetings.

Paper fatigue

When you have so much unread material that you begin to feel as though you cannot cope, you experience 'paper fatigue': a sense of exhaustion when you go near your desk. This has more to do with perception that with reality. The more effectively you prioritize and organize reading, the faster you get through it. New information becomes manageable.

How to prioritize and organize reading?
* put time aside
* do the five-step process (see Chapter 5) on your in-tray every day.

This will guarantee that your in-tray never overflows, you always find what's relevant first, you easily identify what you can throw out and any emergencies can be dealt with without delay. Information overload and paper fatigue most often result from what you imagine to be real rather than what is real. Clear your workspace and deal with the facts before your imagination takes over.

4

how do you avoid information overload at home?

One of the damaging myths of our society is that most information overload is experienced outside the home. The truth is that the home environment is prone to more overload and related stress because the data managed there is more personal and as a result, there is more to lose. Additionally, often there is only one individual responsible for everything that takes place in those walls from child care to cooking, cleaning, financial management and providing the family with an apparently 'stress free' environment.

Parenting, whatever the books say, is one of the most challenging roles we take on as human beings and to undermine it by suggesting the overload and related stress is somehow less than that experienced in the workplace is naive. As discussed in the opening chapter, the key to success in beating information overload is choice. The trick is being able to make the right choice.

Decide what is important: the 'oily beam' test

Imagine you and I are standing at opposite ends of an empty room, approximately ten metres apart. Starting at your end and ending at mine, I draw two parallel lines about half a metre apart. I say to you that if you can walk between the two lines towards me you can have the £10 in my hand. No tricks. All you need do is walk. Would you do it? Probably.

Next, we put two chairs in the room, one at your end of the room and the other at mine. Then get a very strong piece of wood, ten metres long and half a metre wide. Secure each end on either chair. I stand at one end, you at the other. If you walk along the plank, without falling, you can have the £20 I have in my hand. No risk, no danger.

Now imagine you are out of the room. Think of two very tall buildings in a city that you know. We are on top of them, standing at least 50 storeys high. You are on one and I am on the other. A steel 'I' or 'H' beam, about half a metre wide, is placed between the buildings and is securely bolted at each end. I invite you to walk along the beam. You have to walk upright, and you have to stay on the beam. If you were to fall off you would very probably die. Would you do it for £50? Would you do it for £500 or £5,000? How much would I have to offer before you will cross that beam? A million? Ten million? Not at all?

We now know how much money would get you to walk along the beam. Let's complicate it now. It has suddenly become dark. The wind is gusting. It is beginning to rain. There is a fine film of oil on the beam. Now, you have to cross the oily, wet beam in windy conditions, remaining upright. Would you do it? For £50, £5,000, £5,000,000, £20,000,000? Or would all the money in the world not tempt you?

Now, take a moment to think about the *really* important things in your life: family, friends, careers, homes, possessions, dreams, things that are important to you.

So you are on the top of the building, I am on the other. The wet, oily beam is between us. The wind is blowing. I have a large bag in each of my hands. The two things you value most highly are in those bags. You have 30 seconds to cross the beam or one is taken away from you forever. I get to choose which one. Would you cross?

Go through your list. Imagine that I am holding your family in one hand and your friends in the other, which would you choose? Imagine I have your career in one hand and your family in the other, which would you choose? Imagine I have your career in one hand and your dreams in another, which would you choose? Imagine I have your dream job in one hand and your home in another, which would you choose? As you go through your list you will be able to organize your values in a way that shows you what is most or least important in your life. When you build your future, consider your values. Remind yourself of what is important to you. Stick to those and you cannot go far wrong.

Decide what's important – prioritise your time and decide what information you need to support life rather than mould your life around the information that bombards you.

Achieve balance

If it seems to you that you don't have time for anything and are stressed as a result, it will certainly be worth your while to review how you spend your time and determine whether the actual things that you do each day are consistent with your values. Sometimes, you can be pulled into doing what you think you should do instead of what you want to do (for example, allowing work to totally take over your life!). The key thing to remember is that you have choice. The closer your activities are to your core values, the more rewarding the result will be.

Which sounds better to you: choosing how much time you are going to allocate to each event or choosing what events you want to fill your time? Or is it a mix of both?

You have no choice about how much time you have. You do have a choice about how many events you fit into the time you have. The following activity will help you identify which of your typical activities correspond to your values and will help you decide if you are spending your time well.

1 Make a pie chart like that in Figure 1. Divide it into sections that show how you spend your available time (waking hours) during a typical week. If you want to, subdivide the work section with the categories of your work activities.

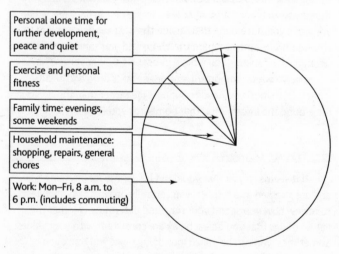

Figure 1 *Example of a time management pie chart.*

2 Now, build your own. This chart should represent how you presently spend your time during a typical week.

3 Once you have completed your pie, return to the 'oily beam test' outlined above and place each activity or category of activities on the beam to determine what is really important to you and nearest your values.

4 Once you have done that, divide the next circle according to your values and compare the two circles i.e. how much time you spend focused on what's important to you versus the time you spend on activities that are of little value to you.

5 Although it may not always seem like it, you do have a choice. You can always say 'no', you can say 'yes', you can say 'maybe'.

Fitting life and dreams together

One of the most important things about time management is reality. When you dream and plan you can be as boundless as you like. When you act on your dreams you need to be realistic. Your actions take place in the real world. It is important to know that you can achieve a great deal in a short amount of time if you manage your events carefully.

Planning and preparation is the key to managing life and information overload. Whether organizing your day or an entire project, the same principles apply:

1 Decide what you want to do.
2 Determine how much time you want to give to each act, task or vision.
3 Plan as much detail as you can, including possible contingency plans.
4 Take action – one at a time, completing tasks as you go.

Planning strategy for fitting it all in

If you have a demanding job and a full family life and still have other projects, it will take careful planning to make it happen. I have used the system described below for many years. It works. Most people with full lives use some form of planning system. Many people only take into account their work activities, and wonder why the other aspects of their life seem neglected. This system accounts for *all* your time and *all* the events you want in your life.

1 Review the 'oily beam' test pie chart allocating your time. Make a list of your different roles and projects, e.g. family, social, job related, hobby, holiday plans, special project, personal development, financial management, etc.
2 Based on the future you want to create, determine the outcome you want to achieve for each item on the above list over a period of four to six weeks (I found four weeks was not quite long enough while six weeks gave me time to do what I wanted).

3 Allocate time for mental and physical holiday times (breaks and breathers).

4 Next to each activity on the six-week list, jot in the approximate time you want to spend on the job and when you are going to do it. Write this in pencil because you will find that things change.

5 Then, in your daily planning system (or whatever system you use), divide your day in half: work related events and non-work related events. In the 'to-do' part of the planner write in all the activities from your six-week list that are due to be done on that day. Make sure that you only put in what you can fit in to the time available.

Evaluation

At the end of each week, month or six-week period, go back to your plans and evaluate how you did. Measure this by reviewing what you did during the period. Where are you giving yourself too much or too little to do? Refer to your pie chart. How are you spending your time? What is not getting done? Does it really matter? Does it reflect your values? Are you getting everything done?

This system will help you ensure that you plan and design how you will achieve your dreams by carrying out concrete, specific action to make them happen. Well managed time, means well managed events within the time available.

Important

Let your family be responsible for their own lives. You don't have to control everything. Back off and give them some space.

5

how do you manage written information?

Occasionally, reading slowly is essential but sometimes, you simply need to get through information, find what you need and clear your in-tray. That is where an effective reading strategy becomes useful.

The five-step strategy outlined in this chapter will allow you to find information quickly, make studying easy, read non-fiction material faster, remember technical and complex material, clear clutter in minutes, process books quickly and easily, apply what you read, read smart and read with a purpose.

As the term implies, speed-reading is about reading fast, but there is more to it than that. For new information to have any value, you need to retain, integrate and apply it. But even before you begin, it's a subject that always raises questions. What is the fastest possible reading speed? How do I remember what I read? How do I maintain concentration when reading difficult material? Is it easy to learn?

If there is a limit on the speed at which people can read, we don't yet know what that limit is. Some people can read a book the size of *War and Peace* in less than twenty minutes and retain and recall enough to answer questions at least as well as those who read 'normally'!

The ability to retain and recall is the most relevant outcome of reading. If you do not intend to remember at least some of what you read, why read it?

The effective reading system described here works by using a five-step process. Follow the guidelines and you will easily and quickly learn to read and manage new information fast and effectively.

Five steps to easy information management

The five-step system is a structured method. It will help you:
* explore the material using at least three different ways
* find information that is relevant to you without missing out what is important
* find the information you require quickly
* integrate new information with what you already know
* accurately recall new information when you need it.

Become familiar with the five-step system. Then adapt it: combine or omit steps to suit your purpose and the style of other non-fiction material (e.g. newspapers, articles, memos, books or magazines).

The five-step effective reading system: organize your reading

If you understand something, it is easier to remember. Imagine reading a book on an unfamiliar subject, or trying to remember material when you don't understand terminology, themes, concepts or jargon. Compare that to remembering new information on a subject you are familiar with.

The purpose of the five-step system is to ensure you:

1 find exactly what you need without having to read irrelevant or unnecessary material
2 never miss relevant information
3 understand, retain and recall information by becoming familiar with structure, content, language and concepts.

For a book of about two hundred pages, Steps 1 to 4 of the system described below could take between five and fifty minutes depending on the depth of information you want. The time for Step 5 will depend on the amount of information you want.

Step 1: Prepare

Preparation should take no more than five minutes.

Lack of focus interferes with concentration and frustrates your reading. By contrast, preparation helps you focus. Your aim is to highlight areas that you want to study and to exclude what you decide is unnecessary.

Establish your purpose and prepare. Ask yourself these questions:

1 What do you *already know* about the subject?
2 What do you *need to know* (is it general information or is it the answer to a specific question)?
3 How and when do you *intend* to use the new information? (Essay, exam or report? General interest? A presentation? When? Next week? Next month? Next year? Or do you need it in ten minutes?)

Step 2: Structure

Take an overview of the material to familiarize yourself with the structure:

* What does it look like?
* How is it organized?
* Are there summaries or conclusions?
* Is the book mainly words?
* Are there pictures?
* What is the print size?
* Is the information organized in sections?

* Is it a series of paragraphs?
* Are there bullet points?

Depending on your purpose, developing an overview of the structure of a two hundred-page book or document should take between one and ten minutes.

During Step 2:
* Read the front and back covers, the inside flaps, the table of contents and the index.
* Scan the bibliography.
* Determine the structure of the book: chapter headings, sub-headings, pictures, graphs, cartoons and images.
* Mark parts of the book that you are sure you will not need.
* Highlight areas you will need.
* Re-affirm your decision: What do you want from the book?

If it does not contain what you need, put the book away. You will save hours of work.

Step 3: Language

You prepared yourself and studied the structure of the book in Steps 1 and 2. Now, familiarize yourself with the *language*. Is there jargon? Is the language complicated? What do the acronyms mean?

It should take five to ten minutes to become familiar with the language of a two hundred-page book.
* Depending on the page size, scan at about a page every two seconds.
* Highlight words linked to your purpose.
* Study the language: Is it technical? Non-technical? User-friendly? Are you familiar with it?
* Do you need to refer to a dictionary?
* Note the meaning of acronyms.

The speed at which you read is determined by your familiarity with the language. Try to recognize recurring themes or concepts during this step. Highlight points that are particularly relevant for your purpose. If necessary, look up key words and concepts before you begin Step 4.

Step 4: Content

Most well-written material outlines the main element of the chapter in the first paragraph. Similarly, the main idea of each paragraph is usually in the first sentence. So read:

* the first paragraph of every section
* the first sentence of every paragraph (if the paragraph is long, read the last sentence)
* summaries or conclusions.

The more thoroughly you highlight, underline, circle, take notes and make spider-graphs of what you read, the easier Step 5 will be.

Step 5: Purposeful selection

By the time you reach Step 5 you will have:

* determined your purpose
* studied the outline and the structure of the material
* read introductions, summaries, and conclusions
* become familiar with language, themes and general contents
* identified sections that contain the information you require.

Now that you are familiar with the book, select *exactly* what you need or want to read.

And now, learn how to read it *fast* ...

Read more words, faster

Most people read at about 150 to 300 words per minute. And here's why: as you read this paragraph, do you hear your own voice in your head 'saying' the words you read? If you do, then you are *reading to yourself*. This happens because of how you were taught to read. It is the reason why you read at the same speed that you speak. It's that simple.

Before you learned to read, you learned to recognize one letter or sound at a time. When you mastered that, you progressed to recognizing one word at a time. You read out loud. That enabled your teacher to check that you recognized and pronounced the words accurately.

Then, instead of reading out loud to yourself, you read silently. You spoke to yourself. That led to a belief that you have to hear every word to comprehend what you read. You don't! Your 'inner voice' became a habit. That's what we're about to change.

You could say that you learned to read with your ears instead of your eyes.

At first you were still learning to recognize the words. 'Reading to yourself' was slow. As your vocabulary increased, you recognized words more quickly. Your reading rate increased until it stabilized at the same words per minute at which you speak. **But your reading strategy did not change**.

The aim is to help you change that strategy: to change the old belief that you have to read with your ears.

Read with your eyes

To increase your words-per-minute reading rate you must accelerate your reading speed until you transform the old habit of sounding out the words in your head (often referred to as sub-vocalization).

Two methods for achieving this are:

1 The guide
   * Place a guide (pen, pencil, or finger) underneath the first or second word of a line.
   * Move the guide smoothly across the page from the beginning of a line to the end of that line.
   * Repeat on each line.
   * Move the guide a little faster than is comfortable.
   * The movement needs to be smooth and swift.

If you pause the guide, you are *following* your eye instead of *leading* it. If you sub-vocalize, your speed will not increase. When the guide moves quickly and smoothly, your eyes are forced to follow. Your reading rate will increase. The faster you move the guide, the less you will sub-vocalize. Your inner voice will be unable to keep up. The aim is to eliminate the habit of reading one word at a time and to stop your attention wandering.

Speed-reading is a skill. It is easy to learn. Developing that skill does not mean you have to read fast all the time. Technical content, print size, mood, familiarity with the subject material and your purpose can affect reading speed. The ability to read quickly allows you to choose how fast or slow you want to read.

2 Selective reading

When you read material on a familiar subject and you don't want to miss out important items in the text, use this technique.

* Read the first sentence of the paragraph.
* Skim the rest of the paragraph for key words, and only if you think it's necessary.
* Read the last sentence of the paragraph.

Concentration

1 Know your purpose.
2 Use a guide, especially if you are tired or if the material is challenging.
3 Make notes as you read.
4 To help maintain concentration, take a break every thirty minutes for approximately five minutes.

If your attention drifts easily, seemingly inconsequential things distract you, and you find it hard to concentrate, an easy solution may exist.

The following will help increase your concentration and your ability to focus on one task.

* To ensure peak concentration, **take breaks often** – approximately five minutes every thirty minutes if you are only reading. If you are reading a number of different texts and taking notes, you could stretch your reading time to between forty-five minutes and one hour before you take a five- or ten-minute break. Pay attention to

your body as you read. When you start yawning, making mistakes, rereading passages or if you develop a headache, it is time for a break. If you work through the symptoms of tiredness, your concentration and your ability to remember and understand what you are reading will diminish rapidly. Taking a break does not mean lying down and going to sleep for twenty minutes (although that does help) – go for a walk, drink some water, do something different.

* Know your **reasons for reading**. The clearer your purpose, the easier it will be to concentrate even if you do not really want to. If you have no reason, however, you will probably give up fairly quickly.

* **Read actively** using a pacer, especially if you are feeling tired or if the material is challenging. The more senses you use, the more alert you are likely to remain. Imagine eating a meal with only the sense of sight. You couldn't smell it, taste it, feel the texture of the food or hear the sounds of cutting and slicing a juicy dish. All you could do was see it and eat it. How much do you think you would enjoy that meal? Most of the enjoyment is in the sensory appreciation of the meal: the taste, smell, texture and presentation of the food. The same applies to reading. Unfortunately we are taught at a very early age to appreciate reading only through *one* sense. When you start building spider-graphs, taking notes, thinking, discussing and actively reading, you will find that reading becomes more like the meal you can see, taste, smell, hear and feel. You almost always remember a good meal when the company is good and the surroundings pleasant. Treat reading like a good meal – you'll be surprised.

* Set a definite **time limit**. Break your reading into chunks. The chunks should be small enough to feel easily managable and big enough to feel that you are achieving your goal. Be realistic. If, as you read, you find that the size of the chunks is too big or too small, stop and reassess. Be flexible.

* The better your **vocabulary**, the faster your reading. To improve comprehension, underline unfamiliar words during Step 3 of the five-step effective reading system (Language). Look up the words at the end of the paragraph, page, and section as appropriate.

Work distractions

Plan your day

Distractions come easily when you don't know what you want to achieve. At the start of your day write down everything you want to achieve, including the reading you want to do. Set aside time for it. It might also be useful to put time aside in your plan for leisure reading. Once you plan it and you can see that reading a novel for a while isn't going to mean that you will not achieve everything else in your day, you will find that you enjoy the time, still get everything done and improve your speed-reading by reading more.

Set ground rules

Once you start something, don't let anything distract you from completing it unless there is a very good reason. Have you ever started mowing the lawn or doing the dishes only to get distracted by something else and then you don't really want to go back to it? Once you start something, *finish it*. This will not only improve the quality of your work, it will increase the quantity of what you can achieve. You will also feel more relaxed and at ease because the job has been done.

People demanding your attention

Few people have the luxury of being able to work without interruptions. There will always be someone, somewhere, demanding your attention at some point, whether by phone, in person or by email.

If you can, set aside the time you need to read and put up a 'do not disturb' notice.

If you are unable to do that, and most of us are, deal with interruptions like phone calls and people wanting to see you by consciously breaking off from your reading task and paying attention to the interruption.

If the phone rings or someone comes up to you while you are reading:

* If possible, finish the sentence or paragraph you are on.
* Place a mark at the place where you stopped.
* Briefly revise in your mind or on paper your understanding of the last sentence you read.
* Then, give attention to the next task.

Once the interruption is over, you can return to your reading:

* Sit for a moment and recall your understanding of the last sentence you read.
* Re-affirm your intention and purpose for reading.
* Set the time again for a manageable chunk.
* Continue to read.

Habit dictates that when we are interrupted we are very likely to 'hop' from one task to another. Instead of doing this, take a brief pause between tasks to ensure that you don't waste time trying to find where you left off before the distraction. Doing this will prevent you from having to sort out your ideas and remove confusion from your mind when you get back to the task.

Clearing your desk of distractions

Mail

If you get a lot of mail at the beginning of the day, have a routine of twenty minutes maximum each day to open all your mail and file it, deal with it or bin it. Don't let anything get in the way of doing that. It might not seem an important job at the time but when a week's mail piles up on your desk undealt with, it can be very distracting and waste more time than a short amount of stress-free time spent every day.

Desk space

Every piece of paper on your desk will distract you several times every day. To minimize this type of distraction, make sure that the only things on your desk are those that have something to do with the project at hand. If you have your 'in' and 'out' trays on your desk, find another place for them for a week. At the end of the week, assess how differently you spend your time. As long as the tray is on your desk, you only have to look up and you will see everything else you have to do that day instead of being able to focus on *one* job at a time.

Clutter

If your desk tends to be full of paper, clear it of *everything* other than the job at hand – for just one day – and see the difference. At the end of each day, make sure you leave your desk totally clear. In the morning you will feel far more relaxed and able to choose what you want to deal with instead of having to deal with whatever happens to be on the top of the pile.

Other people's reading

Do not let anyone put anything on your desk that you haven't seen and agreed to have there, *especially* if you have to read it. When someone gives you something to read, ask them to explain clearly why they think you have to read it, then decide if you want to accept it as an activity in your schedule. If they cannot give you a satisfactory reason, think carefully before you accept it because once you have, you will have to commit the time required to doing it.

6

how do you deal with verbal overload?

The difficulty with verbal information is that if you miss what someone says, it's probably gone forever. You can rarely ask for a re-run just because you drifted off. But when information is coming at you too fast it's not easy to stay focused, especially if the information is dull.

Short of making a recording, taking notes, asking someone to slow down or simply giving up, there's not a lot you can do if someone is going to bombard you with information regardless of whether you're paying attention or not. What you can do something about is making sure you're not the cause of verbal overload. Before you launch into a monologue, whether it's a speech, a lecture or a set of instructions, ask yourself what might switch your listener off? Then don't do it!

It's not a two-way street. You are responsible for maintaining your audience's attention.

Perform at your best even when you are stressed with overload

Performance anxiety can happen in any situation where you have to perform: contributing to meetings with colleagues, speaking on stage in front of several thousand strangers, or sitting an exam. Regardless of the context, the symptoms of performance anxiety include clouded vision, blurred thinking, weak knees, excessive perspiration and weak lips to the extent that you think you would drool if you could summon up enough moisture. Then there is the activity in your head, concern whether your zips and buttons are fastened, if there is loo roll stuck to your shoe. These are symptoms of performance anxiety. Whatever, take a step back, breathe and relax.

Focusing on yourself and what your audience might be thinking about you, rather than what your audience needs and what you want to say to them, causes most performance anxiety and mental overload.

Consider these questions during preparation. The answers will help you generate the right attitude for a great performance:

* What do you want to have happen as a direct or indirect result of the material you will present?
* What message do you want your audience to receive?
* Have you imagined yourself in their place?
* What actions do you want them to take?
* What specific changes do you want to have happen as a result of your message?
* What response do you want from your audience *during* your message?
* What language is your audience accustomed to?
* What mood will your audience be in before, during and after you speak?
* What *other* messages might your audience be receiving at the same time as yours?

* What concerns might your audience have as a result of your message?
* What questions might your audience have?
* How will you present or deliver appropriately to reach out to everyone in the audience?

DO NOT think about yourself – your audience doesn't really care about you. What they want is the message. You are merely delivering it. If you think about yourself, you will be preoccupied with 'stuff' about which your audience has no interest. They want the message, then they want time and space to make decisions about it. They don't want to have to feel sorry for you. If that is what you want then that is all you will get, and they will not *listen* to what you have to *say*.

Adrenalin is good. It sharpens your thinking and your reactions. Fear undoes everything and increases the cortisol dose. Most audiences want to see a speaker succeed. Even if you speak to an audience that would prefer to shoot you down, the calmer you are, the less likely they are to succeed.

Preparation

The loss of focus before or during a performance is usually due to lack of preparation. The frustrating thing about preparation is that the more time you have to prepare, the more time you have to generate fear. When preparing, prepare your mental attitude for the event as well as what you will say and do.

* When you speak, you *own* the space. Invite your audience into it. Your audience is there by your invitation.
* Really get to know and understand your message.
* Talk about your message to other people – not in the form of a prepared speech, rather in conversation.
* Be *passionate* about what you want to say. Excitement wins audiences. Period. It automatically focuses your mind on what you are saying instead of fears you might otherwise have had.

Jokes

Don't include jokes in your presentations unless you:

* know the audience
* are absolutely sure that no one will be offended
* make the joke specific to them
* understand the audience culture: different companies
  and even departments within in the same company have
  different cultures – a joke that works for one legal firm
  might not work for another
* ensure a laughing start is appropriate
* have confidence in your ability to deliver the punch line
  successfully.

If you are concerned about your ability to deliver the joke at
the start of your presentation, your follow through might suffer.
Even good jokes will fail if you flummox the follow-up. *Never* tell
a joke for the sake of it. An impromptu comment in keeping with
the event has a better chance of making the audience smile than
a joke you prepared weeks ago with no prior knowledge of the
audience.

If you are in any doubt how a joke would be received, the
simple rule is to leave jokes to professional comedians.

However ...

Laughter is important. It helps to generate a constructive
atmosphere. A good honest laugh from you or the audience relieves
tension, calms nerves, clears heads and helps audience bonding so
that if you require them to interact in any way or ask questions,
there is a greater likelihood that they will.

If you don't know the audience, have several openings prepared.

Don't stick to your plan too rigidly

If the needs of your audience change during the event, for
instance, if they receive unexpected information that affects them,
be flexible enough to change what you intend to say to blend with
them. If a previous speaker has pre-empted part of what you had

intended to say, adapt your material to suit. If a previous speaker has contradicted what you are going to say, respond appropriately to the contradiction. If you have something more interesting, include it.

However ...

Keep to the core of your message. Don't be influenced into changing *all* of what you intended to say by what someone else says. Get *your* message across.

Don't be tied down by notes

Audiences dislike being presented with the top of a speaker's head as he or she reads a carefully prepared essay word for word. Such speakers are afraid of being distracted by the audience and losing their place. Reading from an essay bores an audience because the lack of eye contact prevents them from interacting with the speaker. Compared with speaking and communicating directly with the audience, the tone of voice while reading is impersonal and monotonous. Also, when a speaker reads a pre-prepared speech, they do not think!

However ...

If you are worried about notes there are other, more effective, ways of prompting yourself though the speech.

* Use a spider-graph. These are excellent for providing all the information you need, on one page, in colour. The good thing about working from a spider-graph is that you can be interrupted any number of times and you will not lose the place.
* When you build your spider-graph, make provisions for using overhead, flip-chart or computer presentation systems. These will prompt you as you speak at the same time as building a picture of what you say for your audience. This will keep them interested and involved. *Avoid* bullet point after bullet point written out so that all you do is read from the screen. They will be justifiably bored and irritated. They are, after all, able to read faster than you can speak.

* Know your subject well enough so that you only need a few words to remind you of what you want to say. Then you can speak fluently from genuine knowledge.
* Use your audience to build your speech. If you intend to answer audience questions, converse with the audience and find out their questions beforehand. Structure what you say around the questions gathered. This lets you remove rhetoric and get to the point. Your audience will appreciate that.
* Use imagination. If you must use essays, write a good one in preparation, then summarise it in a spider-graph.

Don't get your audience to join in too early

If you speak to a general audience – especially a large one – avoid asking for audience responses at the very start of your presentation without carefully thinking about a strategy for ensuring a response. Most audiences are lazy. They want to hear what you have to say and for you to create a good atmosphere in which they will happily participate, if they choose to.

However …

The more you involve your audience, the easier it will be for them to accept difficult information, ask questions or join in later. Most people are nervous about speaking out in public and would prefer not to speak from the audience. The same performance anxieties apply whether you speak from your seat in the audience or from the stage. So when you ask for comments from the audience, especially if they were not pre-warned, don't be surprised at the lack of volunteers.

Involvement technique

1 Before the audience arrives, put flip-chart pens at their seats and pin large pieces of paper on the walls. Put up enough paper for two to ten people to work at each sheet.
2 Draw a vertical line down the middle of each sheet. At the top of the left side write the heading, 'What do you already know about (your subject)?' and on the other half write, 'What questions do you have about (your subject)?'

3 Get the audience to answer these two questions at the start of your presentation. Avoid 'fancy' introductions. The sooner they speak among themselves and ask each other questions, the more involved and interested they will be in the material you present.

4 When you give instructions specify two rules: 1) they can't say 'nothing' on the 'what do you know' side and 2) they must fill the page with normal sized print (the reason for this is that they will try harder – if you tell them to write only a couple of points down, they will literally write two points).

5 While they are filling the sheets, go and meet each group, speak to them, get them to explain and discuss their questions. This will create a noise in the room. A buzz.

6 When they have no more questions, seat them. Tell them that they will, at the end of the presentation, have the opportunity to check that their questions have all been answered.

The aim is to get them to speak up without having to stand out. I use the involvement technique described above at most events. It has worked every time so far. It works particularly well if you are speaking about a technical subject or teaching a new skill.

This strategy does several things:

1 The audience interacts with you and with each other.

2 You can discover how much they know already and what they need to know.

3 It generates a relaxed, safe environment (no one feels forced to stand out).

4 It makes the event relevant to the audience. This will help you gain their attention.

5 When you ask, 'Does anyone have any questions?' at the end of the presentation, you won't be met with silence because your audience will have already gathered all the questions they want answered and are, at this stage, accustomed to contributing.

6 Because you know their questions from the outset, you will know whether you have answered them successfully.

7 The audience will appreciate that the information you present will benefit them and you will gain their trust.

Don't apologise at the beginning

Never start a presentation with 'I'm not going to bore you for long', 'Sorry if I seem nervous but I am' or 'I'll be quick so someone more interesting can speak'. If you want sympathy, go to someone who cares. It's brutal, but true. Your audience does not care. In fact, when you start a presentation saying how boring or nervous you are, you will lose most of your audience. They do not want to listen to someone make excuses. Telling the audience will not make your nerves go away. And if you truly believe that you bore your audience, why speak at all?

However ...

No, however. Just get on with it. If the subject is boring, *make it interesting*. If you are passionate, boredom and nerves will disappear.

* Think before you speak.
* As the meeting progresses, take notes to remind you of your thoughts.
* Don't be bullied into responding to comments or suggestions.
* Don't let anyone threaten you, emotionally, physically, intellectually or psychologically.
* Stick to the facts and don't get emotional.

Impromptu speeches: seven steps in seven minutes

For most people, a prepared speech and contributing at meetings are easy compared with being asked to give an impromptu speech. One of two things may fill your mind when you are asked to speak with no notice: first, nothing at all, your mind goes totally blank; second, mental overdrive. To prevent either mental block, relax and clear your head using one of the relaxation techniques in Chapter 2. Then, use the following strategy to create a structure around which to build a clear and balanced speech.

Step 1: 30 seconds
Calm down, breathe and focus your mind on the specific topic you will be speaking about.

Step 2: 30 seconds
On a piece of paper, write the title of your speech in one clear sentence.

Step 3: 1 minute
Either as a spider-graph or linearly, write between three and six main topics you will want to cover during your speech (if you are being asked to speak without notice it is unlikely you will have to speak for long – four points will generally be enough).

Step 4: 1 minute
Write two sub-points for each of the main topics.

Step 5: 2 minutes
Briefly develop each point.

Step 6: 1 minute
Write a conclusion.

Step 7: 1 minute
Write an introduction.

For a two-minute speech on 'Information Overload', the process would be something like this:

Step 1: Breathe, relax and clear your mind.

Step 2: Write 'Information Overload' on a piece of a paper.

Step 3: Four key points on information overload:
- Definition of information overload
- Reasons for information overload
- Main challenges when trapped by information overload
- How to avoid information overload and create balance

Step 4: Two sub-points for each of the key points:
- Definition of information overload
  - Mental switch from order to chaos
  - Perception
- Reasons for information overload
  - Perfectionism
  - Denial
- Main challenges when trapped by information overload
  - Stress
  - Consequences of inaction
- How to avoid information overload and create balance
  - Work/life balance
  - Regaining perspective

Step 5: Build each point by adding detail to each of the above sub-points.

Step 6: Write your conclusion by briefly summarising the key points.

Step 7: Write your introduction by outlining the main topics you will be speaking about.

Remember, if you feel unqualified to speak on a subject at short notice, say so.

What if you were the world authority on your subject? How would your demeanour, attitude, body language, tone and dress change? How would you treat your audience differently? How interested would your audience be in your subject if you were truly interested?

7

how to remember what you need to remember

One of the first mental faculties to suffer under pressure is memory. This chapter includes techniques on how to remember what you need to remember, when you need to remember it; keep a clear head under stress; remember people; recall under pressure.

Memory is central to everything we do from meeting new people to learning new information. With so much practice our memories should be excellent. Instead, many complain that not only is their memory not good enough, but it's getting worse! The good news is that developing a strong memory is easy and doesn't include practising complicated mnemonics.

A good memory is one of the best signals that you're not suffering from information overload. If you're stressed, frustrated or generally bogged down with life, your memory will suffer. However, rather than the amount of information being the major contributing factor to memory difficulties, it's our attitude towards it.

Maintaining a good memory

Memory is key to everything we do: meeting people, learning new information, planning your day. With so much practice, our memories should be excellent. Instead, many complain that not only is their memory not good enough, it's getting worse!

The good news …

1 Developing a strong, reliable memory is easy.

2 You don't have to practise complicated mnemonics.

3 The more relaxed you are the better your memory will become. So roll out the yoga mat and book a massage!

A good memory is one of the best signals that you are not suffering from overload. If you are stressed, frustrated, angry, fearful or bogged down with life, your memory will suffer. You may be forgetting names, appointments, conversations or what someone just told you a moment ago.

Rather than the amount of information being the major contributing factor to memory difficulties, it is our attitude towards it.

Memory principles

* Memory is not a stand-alone system; it relies on attention, perception and reasoning.
* Memory is not a system based on isolated facts. Everything you remember is interconnected to other information in memory.
* Memory retrieval relies greatly on association. The better organized you are, the more organized your memory will be and the easier it will be to recall information.
* New information is not stored separately from old information. Old knowledge helps make sense of new information and vice versa (one reason why it is easier to read material you know something about).
* Memory is not only for storing information, it is designed for use.

* We speak about memory as if it were an object. We describe ourselves as having a 'good', 'bad' or 'average' memory, in the same way as 'good' or 'bad' lungs. Your memory is not a *thing*. It is certainly not a *single* thing. It is a series of processes taking place in your brain, all the time.
* Your memory can be trained. It has been said that there are no good or bad memories, just trained or untrained. Barring organic damage, with few exceptions, everyone's memory can be developed.
* One common excuse for not wanting to improve memory is, 'I'm too old!!!' If your mind and body are healthy, age is no excuse.
* The more you use your memory the stronger it will become. Many memory problems that people encounter as they become older are due to lack of mental exercise, lack of physical exercise, poor nutrition and excess stress.
* A basic guideline for improving memory and ability to concentrate is to focus on physical and mental health: what is good for the body is also good for the mind.
* A major factor in memory failure is stress.
* Memory includes long-term memory, short-term memory, very short-term memory, kinaesthetic memory, recall, retrieval, recognition, storage … If any one part of this process is not functioning well, your memory will be working below optimum. There is little point absorbing material without a retrieval mechanism.
* One final fallacy is that by memorising too much, you will fill up your brain.

Before we discuss improving your memory, consider how your memory works.

Short-term, intermediate and long-term memory

Short-term memory holds information for seconds and then it is lost. Without short-term memory every piece of information you see, hear, smell, touch or taste would be instantaneously remembered and accessible. This could make gathering new information very difficult. If you want what is in your short-term memory to be available for later recall, you have to pay attention to it and take action to remember it for a longer period of time.

Intermediate memory is retained for typically two to four hours. Have you ever decided to remember something interesting, and then several hours later have not been able to recall what it was? This is intermediate memory. As soon as information is no longer required, it is discarded. This is one reason why you forget people's names. You meet them once, they are remembered while you see them. After the event you might not think about them for a while. Next time you meet them, because your visual memory is stronger than your auditory memory, you might remember where you met them and what they were wearing, but you may not be able to recall their name.

Long-term memory is what people complain about most often. In reading, for instance, your short-term memory retains information long enough for you to make sense of the sentence or paragraph you are reading. Intermediate memory retains information long enough so that you can make sense of the chapter. Long-term memory helps you remember and make sense of the whole book. Long-term memory requires revision and application.

Long-term memory works with short-term and intermediate memory. As you might imagine, the three systems are interconnected. Gaps or weaknesses in one of them will prevent the whole system from working effectively.

How memory works – and when it doesn't – a simple model

There are many models that attempt to explain how the memory system works. Basically, your memory is divided into three parts:

* **Acquisition** – absorbing information via sensation, perception and interpretation

* **Retention** – keeping it in your head
* **Retrieval** – getting it out again.

A memory can become unavailable at any point. The trouble is, you only know it is unavailable when you try to retrieve it: you are in the company of someone whose name you have forgotten, unable to introduce them to someone (whose name you have also forgotten!).

There are some basic rules that will help you improve your memory:

Four steps to memory acquisition

Pay attention

Most of the time you 'forget' something because you deprived yourself of the opportunity to remember it in the first place. Have you ever been introduced to someone then several seconds later you realize you have 'forgotten' their name? Chances are your attention was somewhere else – you were not present.

Plan

Before you begin, think forward to when you will be likely to use the information. In what context will you use it? What state will you be in (calm, excited, nervous) when you want the information (exam conditions for instance)?

Be interested

Even if the event seems dull, find something in or about it that interests you. If you are bored, parts of your brain will not be involved and this will make paying attention even more difficult.

Be active

Think about what you are doing. Your memory does not work in isolation. The more connections you make between the new and old information the easier it will be to understand and integrate. Understanding and integration are key to remembering.

Memory retention (storage)

Storing information in your head is one thing, storing it in such a way that you can retrieve it later is a different matter.

Your memory thrives on association and order. The better organized your memory, the easier it will be to retrieve information when you need it. You do not have to keep everything in your head. Be organized on paper and you will know where to find the information when you need it.

Memory needs rehearsal and revision so that it may be effectively retained and recalled. There are several ways to achieve this. The least effective is rote rehearsal: as soon as the memory is interfered with, the information disappears. For instance – if someone gives you a telephone number and then asks where you put your keys, the telephone number will fade. The loss of the keys will take your mind on a search. You will be attending to that instead of trying to store the number.

The more mental time you spend on thinking about and understanding what you are trying to remember the better chance you will have of remembering it.

Memory retrieval

Memories are stored in several parts of your brain. When you recall your memory of your front door, several areas of your brain will be activated. You might simultaneously:

* see an internal picture of your door (visual)
* hear the sound of it closing (auditory)
* recall the last time you walked through it (kinaesthetic and proprioceptive)
* remember the feeling of the last time you locked yourself out (emotional)
* smell the fresh coat of paint when you painted it last (olfactory).

When we try to retrieve information we often use only one access point. If you can re-create the whole experience as you remembered it, it will be easier for you to recall further information. One reason we have difficulty retrieving information is that the retrieval method is inappropriate.

Depending on how the information was originally presented to you, there are different types of memory retrieval. The easiest information to remember is information you can easily recognize and fit into an existing schema or framework. Recognizing a face is sometimes easier than remembering the name that goes with it. When you are looking for information you have read previously you might say that you know where it is, you can see it on the page and when you find the page, you recognize the text, you just cannot recall the actual piece of information itself.

Recall is when you are given no clues at all. As opposed to *recognizing* a face, you have to *recall* their name. Most information that you forget is the information you have to recall.

Forgetting

We often become aware of our memories only when we forget something. Memory failure can happen because of disorganization, distraction or lack of awareness.

Studying the difficulties that people have when recalling information can help us understand how our memories work. Memories are often available (we know we have read it, or seen it, we can remember where we were when we remembered it in the first place) but the actual information is not accessible (just cannot quite remember it fully). This phenomenon is called 'tip of the tongue'. Most psychologists think that long-term memory is organized in categories, and these categories are linked, much like a spider-graph. One thing reminds you of the next and so on. If these links change or become damaged in any way then the information might become inaccessible. You might forget it entirely. 'Forget' in this sense means that you are unable to reconstruct the information.

Factors contributing to forgetfulness

Lack of attention (the pickpocket effect)

Problem: If you pay full attention to a task, you will not notice other things going on around you. While it might seem like a contradiction, daydreaming is one of the few activities we carry out with full attention. Next time you notice your mind wander, notice how much of your surroundings you were paying attention to.

Did you notice the normal noise around you or see people moving about?

Workaround: Improve your concentration. Chapter 5 can help you with this.

Interference

Problem: Interference can be retroactive or proactive. When you change your telephone number the new one somehow 'latches' onto your memory and replaces the old one. This is called *retroactive interference*. It comes from new information. *Proactive interference* is when old information interferes with new information. Thinking of your telephone number again, this is when you cannot remember your new one because your old number keeps coming into your mind instead.

Workaround: To work around retroactive and proactive interference, rest between different stages or pieces of work. This allows time for your mind to consolidate new information, to separate old information and integrate new information within the framework of your existing knowledge (unless it is your telephone number).

Lack of interest or motivation

Problem: Remembering new information is almost impossible without interest or some motivation. Tiredness can contribute to this. Even if you are interested in what you are working on, the interest will fade if you are tired.

Workaround: Find something that motivates you, no matter how small or seemingly unrelated. The task must benefit you in some way or another. Take breaks as often as you feel you need them – at least ten to fifteen minutes every hour to hour and a half.

Insufficient links or association

Problem: If the information or job is particularly new to you, making sense of the ideas may be challenging due to your framework being in the early stage of development. If you cannot make sense of the ideas you will find them very difficult to remember.

Workaround: Study the glossary of terminology and any other related topics. This will help develop the mental infrastructure. For example, become familiar with the legends and conversions of a road map or atlas before using a map.

Insufficient revision

Problem: Memories are made of memory traces. If they are not reinforced they will fade.

Workaround: A basic guideline is to revise seven times in ten days, or develop a very good filing system. To remember information in the long-term, use it or lose it.

Stress and memory

Stress destroys memory. Period. When you are stressed you release high levels of the hormone cortisol into your body. Cortisol affects you in a variety of ways depending on the amount released into your body. Cortisol destroys glucose, your brain's *only* source of food.

If you have ever been involved in or witnessed an accident or other trauma, you may have 'got through it', and appeared to be fully conscious. Afterwards you may have been unable to remember anything, or had an inadequate memory about the incident. You would have experienced a level of stress that caused the release of a large amount of cortisol which would have affected the hippocampus area of your brain and destroyed the glucose. With no food your brain literally did not have the necessary materials to lay the long-term memory down. You saw everything. Maybe even walked around and spoke to people. But the memories were not laid down in any form that can be recalled.

It is even more complex than that. If the hormones go into the same configuration at the time of the event, a phenomenon known as 'state dependent memory' can cause flashbacks and behavioural or mood problems. So the memory does get laid down but not in a way that is ordinarily readily available. If you experience such problems after a trauma there are several therapeutic approaches that may help.

A less extreme effect happens if, for example, you are about to give a speech, meet new people, introduce your boss to your partner. You might feel a little fuzziness or other sensation. You know that you know what you should know, but you can't quite get the ideas, names or words correct. It might feel somewhat like a telephone line in a storm. The lines are there, communication should be possible, but there's interference from somewhere.

There is a further scenario in which cortisol affects your brain and is damaging in a different way. People who live a highly stressed life have a self-induced, intravenous drip of cortisol into their bodies. This cortisol destroys glucose and turns calcium into free radicals that destroy brain cells. This can cause age-related memory loss. People between age forty and fifty years might feel that they're not thinking as fast and clearly as they once did. Left unchecked these consequences can be permanent. No matter what age you are (and providing there is no organic damage to your memory), or what myth you choose to believe, your memory *will* become clearer, more creative, more active and more accurate if you work at it.

Although there will be no overnight effect, constant and determined action will be rewarded. There is no magic pill for instant memory. If you choose to be, you have the natural capacity to be brilliant. It takes effort, common sense and belief in yourself.

In summary, pressure makes it difficult to remember. The first step to developing a great memory is learning how to cope with stress in situations where you need to remember.

De-stress when you need to remember

Factors that contribute to your stress levels are:
* the amount of information you need to remember
* the time you have available
* your control over the situation
* your confidence in your ability to recall.

When you feel stressed, say 'STOP!' very loudly in your head. Imagine everything around you freezes to a standstill, then take a mental or physical step backwards. Then:

1 Smile, breathe deeply twice (abdominally), stand or sit up straight.
2 Inside your head (or out loud) laugh. A real belly laugh is a superb de-stresser.
3 Ask those around you to slow down.
4 Take your time to answer questions and speak just a little more slowly.
5 Write information down if it's appropriate.

Remember names and faces

One strategy for remembering the names and faces of those you meet is to **prepare, pay attention** and **practise**.

Prepare

Before an event: get the agenda and a guest list, study it and look for names of people who you have met and know well, people you think you have met but can't remember clearly and people you want to meet. Then prepare a strategy for who you are going to meet first. If you want to see the people you know well first, then when you walk into the room, look for the person you want to speak to and go directly to them without making eye contact with anyone else. This will prevent you being ambushed by too many new faces as soon as you arrive and will give you time to become familiar with the room. The best way to gain control is to arrive early to meet the people you want to meet, one at a time.

Pay attention

When two people meet for the first time, natural first impressions happen within the first few seconds. However, while the first impression is developing, you are also being introduced and by the time you introduce yourself, you often realize you didn't catch their name because you didn't hear it. You didn't hear it because your attention was elsewhere.

The first time you meet someone:
* Smile, breathe slowly and abdominally, and take your time.
* Spend enough time with each person you meet (if possible).
* Listen carefully to the name. Say it back to make sure you are pronouncing it correctly.
* Ask the spelling, especially if it's a difficult name or if the person mumbled.
* If the event allows, stick to first names only.
* Pay attention to the whole person: their style of dress, postures, gestures, unique identifying features and how they walk.
* Get a business card.
* Then ...

Practise
* *Use* people's names. Help them by using yours. If you have forgotten their name, ask for it, people will not be offended. If you think they will be, ask someone else for it.
* If someone struggles to remember your name, use it in the conversation '... and I said to myself, Tina, ...'.
* Introduce yourself when you join a group. Don't wait for someone else to do it; they might not.
* Finally, get into the habit of making the introductions.

Ten tips on how to develop a great memory

1 Be present – listen and pay attention to what is going on around you. Most forgetting is the result of not remembering in the first place.
2 During a meeting, keep your mind clear by listening instead of constructing your reply. Write down beforehand what you want to say.
3 Good eating habits, plenty of exercise, a relaxed attitude and sufficient sleep all go a long way to improving your memory. Ginkgo biloba, ginseng and lecithin may help too.

4 The more you use what you want to remember, the easier it will be to recall later.

5 Make yourself memorable by introducing yourself slowly and clearly.

6 The more background information you know about something, the easier it will be to recall. Whether it's about a subject or a person, ask questions about what you want to know.

7 Good focus and concentration is key to good memory.

8 If possible, do one thing at a time.

9 Stick to habits. If you always put your keys in one place, you are unlikely to lose them.

10 Don't be too stressed if you happen to forget something.

Instant tip

You are human. Don't beat yourself up if you forget something. Look instead at why you might have forgotten it and solve the problem from the root cause, up.

8

how do you live life – not just survive day by day?

We don't dream of retiring at sixty or sixty-five anymore. We dream of stopping work as soon as possible giving us all the time in the world to do all the things we want to do with our lives without the restraint of nine to five.

Although information can tie you down and overwhelm you, it can also set you free. As we grow into adulthood, most of us develop an assumption that we know how the world works. For some, life is a struggle; living cheque to cheque, never knowing what's going to hit them next. For others, life seems easy. Instead of wondering what these people are doing differently to make life seem so easy, strugglers carry on struggling as if there's some lifelong competition to see who can bring the most tragic stories to the water cooler. The truth is, there's no need to struggle at all.

The better your information about how the world works is, the easier life becomes. Instead of allowing random information to clutter your mind, take the time to find out what you need to know to live an easy life.

For instance, ours is an economic society. If you're struggling financially, chances are, you're collecting the wrong financial information. Don't put up with struggle. Learn how money works. That's information worth spending some time on.

In this chapter find the information you need to live life rather than survive it:

* Work out what you really want from life and what you need to know to make it happen.
* Plan life instead of responding to crises.
* Put money and debt into perspective.

Financial security and dealing with debt

If your finances are in disarray, you will be distracted subconsciously – and sometimes consciously – before you even begin your daily activities, whether they are work or leisure, from when the mail arrives in the morning, through to when you pay for dinner at night. Have you ever had a feeling of doom when you offer your 'plastic'? Will it be refused? Images of the supermarket queue built up behind you, the cashier tells you the card has been declined. Run? Make an excuse? Leave? Write a cheque? Would they take a cheque? Fear, frustration, embarrassment ...

Are you in the habit of ignoring your finances and hoping that somehow they will have magically put themselves in order? No news is not always good news as far as money is concerned. When the crunches (plural) come, they will not be as easy to sort as they would if you have been 'taking care of business' as you go along.

Examine the facts

Without referring to any bank or credit card statements, get a piece of paper and write on it:

1 The names of *all* debit, credit and store cards you have and:
   a their current balance

    b the exact date that the next payment is due on each

    c how much will be going out of your bank account

2 All direct debits or standing orders on your bank account and:

    a how much each is for

    b when they are due out

3 Your bank balances and:

    a the dates of the next income

    b the amounts of the next income.

When you have done that, get all your latest bank, credit and store card statements. Check how accurate you were.

Could you do it? How close were you? Did you not even start because you didn't have the information in your head?

Fear about money only exists when you don't have the facts. If your finances are in order life is a whole lot easier. There is a very good reason why money is called currency – if you have it you are current. If your finances are in order you can do what you choose to do or need to do free from stress or worry.

There is only one reason why people have money problems – they spend more each month than they bring in. Gradually, the debt problem builds up to a level where the debt outweighs any possibility of paying it off so they get trapped into debt payment systems that charge massive interest and never allow them to really clear the debt fully. For those who are unfortunate enough to be in this position, their finances may look something like the debt trap illustrated in Figure 2.

The ideal scenario is that you clear your debt, reduce your tax burden, allow for unexpected expenses (for instance, vehicle repairs, dental treatment), get the best deals on your general living expenses, and learn how to make your money work for you. This chapter is not a comprehensive guide on how to get financially sorted. What this chapter will do is help you clear your head about your money so you can start to clear it for real. It might give you a much needed jolt that will get you off your backside and moving towards a genuinely secure financial future.

If, after you have sorted your finances, you find you don't have any money, you will still be better off because you will know how

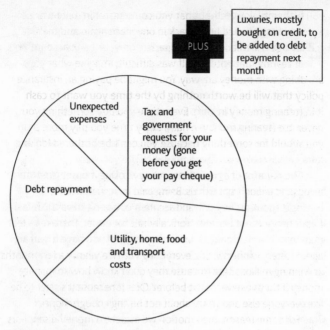

PLUS

Luxuries, mostly bought on credit, to be added to debt repayment next month

Unexpected expenses

Tax and government requests for your money (gone before you get your pay cheque)

Debt repayment

Utility, home, food and transport costs

Figure 2 *The debt trap.*

much you don't have and you are also more likely to do something about it.

Emotional money

Do this *before* you read any further:

1 Get your wallet or purse or whatever you keep your money in.
2 Take out the note of the highest value/denomination.
3 Now, tear it in half.

Have you done it yet? Have you torn it in half? Are you still holding onto it in one piece, saying 'no chance!!'?

What are you feeling at the moment? What's going on in your mind? Are you thinking about the value of the currency you are holding and that if you tore it in half you would lose it? Or did you wait until you realized that you could tear it in half because a piece of tape would put it back in one piece again and make it money again instead of scrap paper?

If tearing that note in half was difficult, imagine what you are doing with money anyway. You might be paying an insurance policy that will be worth nothing by the time you want to cash it in (tearing money in half). Every time you buy something you never use (tearing money in half). Every time you pay more than you should for something because you can't be bothered looking for a better deal (tearing money in half).

We put a lot of emotion into money. Losing it upsets us. Not being paid enough agitates us. Being paid too much worries us. Having it makes us feel safe and secure. Not having it makes us feel frightened and 'not current'. Ironically, not having it can make us feel that we will remain part of something. How often have we heard about lottery winners losing everything within a year or a few months of winning millions? Is it because they don't know how to manage money if they've never had it before? Or is it because it's safer to be like everyone else and worry about not having enough money?

For some reason, the emotion we attach to money disappears as soon as it doesn't look like money anymore. Even credit cards manage to deceive you. Have you ever attempted to buy something to the value of £8, and at the till you are told that they only take credit cards for purchases over £10, so you pick up something you really don't need or want, to make it £10 or more. You won't have to do that often for it to have an impact on your monthly cash flow. Besides, if you were paying cash and were told that you couldn't pay cash for anything less than £10, wouldn't you walk out of the shop? Wouldn't you think you were being manipulated and ripped off? Yes, you would. But, because plastic doesn't hold the same emotional value as cash, you are happy to let yourself be ripped off!

Education

We are the way we are about money primarily because we were never taught to be any other way. We were taught how to earn money – get an education, get a job, get a better education, get a better job, the better your job the higher your salary, and so on. However, the higher your salary, the higher your taxes, the bigger your house, the greater the cost. People in one-bedroom apartments can have more disposable income than those living in penthouses whose disposable income is often disposed of before they even get it! We are not taught how to make money work and we are not taught how to generate an income unless it involves working a full week. We are not taught that living is meant for learning and exploration and expansion, growth, excitement and passion. Instead we are taught that if we have a good job, and earn a good wage, we are a success. Tosh!

There is so much more to life than just working to earn enough to pay taxes and bills. Get your money in order and get your head straight about the value of money and how to make it work. It's much more fun.

Technology is designed for personal financial management. Instead of waiting for your statements to come through once a month, you can use Internet online banking and be fully informed anytime, anywhere about your money.

Wealthy people don't just know how to make money, they know how to spend it and manage it.

Below is a strategy for getting your finances in order. You will appreciate that money is far from the 'root of all evil'. The more you know about your money, the easier it is to make more. It is merely currency; the material that society uses to allow us to exchange goods and services. The more current you are, the more freely you can interact with society at large.

Perhaps more importantly, if you understand your finances, you will be much more confident, you will be less stressed, and, each and every day, you will experience less fear.

Learn about money

Learn how to manage money. Learn how to *make* it as opposed to just earn it. Learn how to spend it and invest it. Learn how to enjoy it. Before that, learn about your current financial position.

Knowing where your money goes

Even though it might seem like a big job, this exercise may be one of the most important you will ever do. Take time out and do it. You will be surprised by what you find. The insight will allow you to manage your expenditure with your 'eyes open'.

1 Gather the last 12 months' bank, store and credit card statements (even if it costs you to get copies).

2 Either on a PC or paper, create a spreadsheet with columns breaking down exactly what goes out each month. Categorise the expenditures according to what they are, i.e. food, clothing, transport, taxes, heating, telephone or electricity bills, dinner out, entertainment, computers and technology, etc.

3 Add up each category; for instance, what you spent on clothing each month for the last year.

4 To get an average expenditure per month through the year for a particular category, divide the number for that category by 12.

   Do this thoroughly and honestly. If you avoid being truthful, you will deceive only yourself.

The reason for this exercise is that although you make a purchase in one month, if you buy on credit, you pay for it for anything from six months to four years later (plus interest). This impacts your cash flow by increasing monthly debt payments and decreasing disposable income and capital.

When a friend of mine did this exercise he found that in that year he had spent an average of £6,000 per month on IT equipment (£72K in the year!) Most of this was bought on credit so the final pay-off was much higher because of very high interest! This included everything: printers, inks, consumables and any other hardware. It did not include paper. He had no idea that so much income was going towards technology that simply seemed like a good idea at the time!

When he was aware of what he was spending his money on, he was able to reduce these outgoings and manage his expenditure more intelligently.

Tearing the note in half showed you how emotionally attached you are to money. You now also have a good idea of where it goes each month.

Open your eyes and clear your mind of financial overload

Money problems are difficult to manage if you don't know what is going on. As hard as it may seem, make yourself aware of your financial situation. Get into a habit of reading and analysing your bank and credit card statements every month. Then do the following:

1 Contact your bank and get a list of all the direct debits and standing orders you have on your accounts and check all of these outgoings against the actual bills.

2 Check all of the life/death insurance policies you have. Contact the company providing them and make sure that what you are paying over time makes financial sense.

3 Check and fully understand *all* your bank charges and other fees the bank takes from your account every month. Banks do sometimes make mistakes; check that they are not over-charging you for anything.

4 Check all the purchases you made on credit. Some credit companies have higher interest rates than others. If you can, increase the payments each month or pay the 'expensive credit' off as early as you can. You will save a lot of interest.

5 Keep the interest payments as low as possible by moving money between cards. Check the rate of interest on your credit cards. Most companies advertise a low interest rate for the first six months. Some offer an ongoing low interest rate even after the initial six months. If you have such a card, use it to keep down your interest. Be proud to be a card tart! But also be careful because it takes considerable effort to keep your eye on the game. Moving money between 0% interest cards has a double-edged benefit; not only will it keep your interest down, but finding, applying for and managing your credit in this way will be so time consuming you might just find it easier to clear the lot and use that energy to invest your money rather than blow it on stuff you don't need.

6 If you automatically pay the full amount on each card every month you should pay no interest at all.

7 Since credit card companies make money from your interest payments and other charges they are often reluctant to help you completely clear the balance each month and thus pay no interest at all. If you want to arrange this, and they will not let you do it, close that account and move to a new credit card company that will. Also, don't take for granted that because you have asked the credit card company to take the full amount each month that they will. In my experience, they seem to conveniently forget instructions like that and charge you the interest anyway!

If you want to be financially literate, then keeping a record of your finances is vital. When you know exactly what your financial situation is, you will have two choices:

1 Adjust your way of life to fit your income.
2 Adjust your income to fit your way of life.

Money and guilt

Have you ever been out with a group of friends for a meal and felt compelled to pay more than your fair share? Or been in the pub and had to buy the first round, which is usually the most expensive since everyone will have one, and has the added disadvantage that the round will probably come back to you before the night is out? Have you ever bought a round and felt annoyed that as a light drinker or teetotaller you are paying for more expensive drinks for everyone else?

This social behaviour stems from our reluctance to talk about pounds and pennies. If everyone were to pay for their share they would have to discuss money. For most of us, it's easier to say, 'I'll get this' instead of 'I'll only pay for my share'.

Instead of being socially bonding this can lead to resentment and damaged friendships.

Starving guilt

Next time you are out in a group, say straightforwardly that you would prefer to pay for your own meal instead of an equal share. You can be diplomatic. Say that you might want something more expensive and don't want others to subsidise you. That allows you to choose what you want, enjoy your meal, stick to your budget and keep your friends.

When someone in a group offers to buy a round, thank them and tell them that you prefer to get your own. That will take you out of the 'loop'.

It won't be easy. There will be pressure to conform. But if you want to get a grip on your money, begin by not letting others spend it for you.

In dealing with money, you will make mistakes. When something goes wrong and it costs you, instead of getting angry, frustrated and fearful that it will happen again, learn from it. Provided you *do* learn from the situation, treat the cost as 'school fees' – paying for an education.

Information overload in a busy world

A successful and proven method of managing non-fiction material is the five-step reading strategy outlined in Chapter 5. If you need to refresh your memory, go back to Chapter 5 and re-read it. In addition to the five-step strategy, there are a number of other techniques you can use to help minimize the unwanted information you are presented with.

Information has the potential to instil terror in the boldest souls: 'If I don't read this/understand this/know this, what will I be missing and what will the consequences be?'

Most of the seemingly infinite information to which you have access to is irrelevant to your purposes. Overloading with 'non-sense' contributes greatly to mental block and overload. I can't overemphasize how important it is to identify, then ignore, irrelevant information.

You are exposed to this risk much more so if you work in a large organization. If you want your desk and your mind to remain clear, develop your ability to identify and prioritize relevance. This will help prevent clutter in your mental and physical spaces and put a barrier up against overload. I say 'put a barrier up' because with every piece of information you are given a choice: accept it, do something with it, attach a consequence to it, add it to your 'maybe later' pile or ditch it.

Choices we make that lead to overload

The 'need to know everything' syndrome will turn your desk into an information bottleneck and take up a huge proportion of your mental and physical time, unnecessarily. Some symptoms and their 'cures' are outlined here:

Apparent urgency: dealing with something as soon as you receive it no matter what else has to be done or how important it really is. If someone gives you a document to read and says, 'This is urgent, you must read it now', don't take their word for it. It may be urgent to them. In your day it might come second or fifteenth. Prioritize all new work and interruptions. Stay on purpose.

Nobody does it better: excellent attitude if you want to work every weekend and most holidays. Most people are capable of doing their jobs well. Think lucky, have faith, prioritize and delegate.

Generosity: when it comes to your own time you cannot always afford to be generous. Often the people giving you something extra to deal with are trying to avoid doing what they have been tasked with. Distinguish between being 'delegated to' versus being 'dumped on'!

Don't accept every piece of information that lands on your desk without establishing:

1 that you are the best person to process the information
2 why you should read it
3 what you are expected to do with it.

Prioritize information

The more effectively you prioritize your reading the faster you will get through it. You will be surprised at how much you can achieve when you enlist the help of others and share information. When unread material piles so high that you feel you can't do anything about it, you will experience a feeling of exhaustion when you approach your desk, commonly known as 'paper fatigue'.

When you prioritize, you are much less likely to become an information bottleneck. If you are starting with a large quantity of unprioritized documents this might take some time. Do it once however, and you will get used to prioritizing and will do it naturally on a daily basis.

To prioritize effectively:

1 Gather all your backlogged reading or paperwork.
2 Sort it into groups:
   a **Urgent:** if you don't deal with/read this, something, somewhere will go drastically wrong – soon.
   b **Important:** if you don't deal with/read this now, the world won't collapse, but if you leave it too long, it might.
   c **Useful:** information that would be good to know, but is not urgent.
   d **Nice to know:** information that is nice have access to, but if you never read it, it wouldn't matter. This might include magazine and newspaper articles you thought looked interesting.
   e **Bin:** bin!
3 Go through each pile, starting with the 'urgent' pile, sort it into **pay-off** or **rip-off**. Will the document make you money (give you value) or cost you money if you do not deal with it? If any documents in the 'urgent' pile do not have a pay-off, perhaps they are not so urgent. Also consider whether they are 'urgent' because someone else said so?
4 Quickly determine how long each document will take to read. Plan the reading into your day according to when you will need the information. Reading something that you will not use for several weeks will mean that you will have to revise it. Date it and read it when it is necessary (sometimes procrastinating is the right thing to do).

If you consistently receive documents that you don't need, it can be annoying and time-wasting. Receiving as little 'junk mail' as possible will help make daily prioritization much easier.